gary soto
a natural man

gary soto

a natural man

CHRONICLE BOOKS
SAN FRANCISCO

Printed in the United States.

Library of Congress Cataloging-in-Publication Data available.

ISBN 0-8118-2518-3

Book design: Michael Osborne Design
Cover illustration: José Ortega

Distributed in Canada by Raincoast Books
8680 Cambie Street
Vancouver, BC V6P 6M9

10 9 8 7 6 5 4 3 2 1

Chronicle Books
85 Second Street
San Francisco, CA 94105

www.chroniclebooks.com

Acknowledgments:
Some of the poems have appeared in the following magazines: *Bellingham
Review, Crazy Horse, Green Mountain Review, The Nation, New American
Writing, Ontario Review, Poetry, Poetry International, Quarterly West,* and
Verse. "Inheritance," "Devising Your Own Time," "Late Confession," "Chitchat
with the Junior League Women," and "Looking for My Brother at the Computer
Factory" appeared in *Poetry.*

THIS BOOK IS FOR NANCY MARQUEZ, ONE OF THE BEST.

Contents

The Mariachi Suit
para José Padilla

I squeeze into the mariachi suit
And walk down East Wino,
Mid-day, my spurs jangling music,
My guitar like a small coffin
In my arms. I knock a knuckle
Against the guitar, the hollow ring
Of a skull. My sombrero is
Huge as the dented lid of a trash can,
And my mustache could sweep all
Of Fresno, it's so responsive to dust.
I attract two cats, tails clicking
With fleas. I attract one
Black brother who asks, "Who you, man?"
I strum my guitar, a rusty clue.
He snaps his fingers and says,
"You Zorro, huh?" I work my fingers
Over D and A, the drunken chords
Of every Mexican bar song.
Brother circles me. He says,
"You Cochise, right?"
I shake my head, sombrero slipping
To the nests of eyebrows.
"You a dude like Pancho Villa!"
He shouts, "Cold day if
You messed with that La Raza Brother!"
I let out a *grito* that starches
The tails of the two cats,
And scares away my brother.
I strum my guitar. I think of
José Alfredo Jiménez, the gravel
He kicked from one Lupita to another,
All the lashes he took like a man

1

From the braided hair of country girls.
Thus, I serenade these cats,
Who yawn, lick the clover pads
Of their salty paws, and prance away.
No one knows me, and no one cares.
I hike up my pants and twist my mustache,
Washerwoman's mop on any other day.
My arms hug the guitar-coffin
With nothing but a drunken heart.

My chalk is no longer than a chip of fingernail,
Chip by which I must explain this Monday
Night the verbs "to get," "to wear," "to cut."
I'm not given much, these tired students,
Knuckle-wrapped from work as roofers,
Sour from scrubbing toilets and pedestal sinks.
I'm given this room with five windows,
A coffee machine, a piano with busted strings,
The music of how we feel as the sun falls,
Exhausted from keeping up.

                    I stand at
The blackboard. The chalk is worn to a hangnail,
Nearly gone, the dust of some educational bone.
By and by I'm Cantiflas, the comic
Busybody in front. I say, "I get the coffee."
I pick up a coffee cup and sip.
I click my heels and say, "I wear my shoes."
I bring an invisible fork to my mouth
And say, "I eat the chicken."
Suddenly the class is alive—
Each one putting on hats and shoes,
Drinking sodas and beers, cutting flowers
And steaks—a pantomime of sumptuous living.

At break I pass out cookies.
Augustine, the Guatemalan, asks in Spanish,
"Teacher, what is 'tally-ho'?"
I look at the word in the composition book.
I raise my face to the bare bulb for a blind answer.
I stutter, then say, *Es como adelante.*
Augustine smiles, then nudges a friend
In the next desk, now smarter by one word.
After the cookies are eaten,

We move ahead to prepositions—
"Under," "over," and "between,"
Useful words when *la migra* opens the doors
Of their idling vans.
At ten to nine, I'm tired of acting,
And they're tired of their roles.
When class ends, I clap my hands of chalk dust,
And two students applaud, thinking it's a new verb.
I tell them *adelante,*
And they pick up their old books.
They smile and, in return, cry, "Tally-ho!"
As they head for the door.

Retired, my grandfather chewed frijoles like a camel,
His large jaw churning,
His tortilla a napkin at the edge of his plate.
He ate alone, or nearly alone,
A parakeet the size of a swollen thumb
Glancing in a mirror. When the parakeet rang its bell,
Grandfather moved his camel head and scolded, "Shaddup."
The bird was not his,
But grandmother's, hall shuffler in pink slippers,
Whipper of rugs and work clothes,
Beautician dying her hair black on shadow-cold mornings.

Nights, grandfather sat in his recliner
With the thorn-sharp doily on his neck.
He sat while the TV shuffled light in his face
And the radio plugged his ears with mariachis.
In the kitchen, the washer shivered a load of whites,
Plates rattled, black tea rolled its knuckles in a sauce pan.
When the telephone rang its loud threats,
He turned his camel head and shouted, "Shaddup!"
He wanted the peace of a green lawn, lost at dusk,
And a summer burst of tomatoes and squash on whiskery vines.
He believed in water, water of morning
And of night, water of sprinklers set at the curb.
He knew how summer heat suckled trees and lawns.
This worried him. How it all could dry up,
Life included, dry up in the time you turned your back
And flicked a grain from under a fingernail.

Grandfather rose late,
The day already sobbing heat in the garden.
He sliced a lemon and in the bathroom
Rubbed its sweet acids under his arms,
The scent that would follow him through the day.

The squeezed lemon collapsed into a frown,
And he was ready. Ready for what? He ate
And drank coffee, his mouth pleated on each deep sip.
He studied his roses, the wicked queens of his garden,
And raked puckered oranges into a herd
Of croquet balls. "Keep things green, *mi'jo,*"
He repeated to me about life.
Water surged in the flower bed
And into the volcanic peaks
Of ant hills, the silt as fine as gold.
Grandfather was a simple man, a work-worn camel
With a busy jaw. Our inheritance was a late afternoon
With my small hand under his, the garden hose splashing
For the good of the living.

I can set the clock five minutes ahead,
Just enough to give me a head start,
A fair chance on my legs that are water and bone.
I could set the clock back, too,
Say seven minutes to nine—I miss a flight
And the plane goes down among Black Angus cows.
In my house, none of the clocks is right,
Each with its own metallic breathing,
Its own oily click of sprockets and spools,
Springs with the leap of a feisty frog.
I keep six watches in our *tansu,*
Occasionally holding them like lizards,
All with their spider-like hands up in surrender.

I tell my wife, I'll cook for you,
And shake my sleeve to examine my Timex.
I throw a pumpkin into a pot,
A pumpkin that I measured with a smile,
Three teeth, a wedge-shaped nose.
I boil this fatboy fruit and lose track,
My mind collapsing like a pumpkin in boiling water.
I pace the house, another measure of time,
My steps like a sick man in a robe.
I watch shade move across the lawn
And a single leaf swing from the poor-postured elm.
These, too, are time, and my cat's meowing at the door.
To tell you the truth, I'm losing confidence.
In my heart, I know it's ten to ten,
That I'm somewhere in my forties,
That the calendar has gutted most of January,
That my watch is panting on my wrist.

Maybe I'll make my flight
And over Iowa grip my armrest, tears
Pulled from my eyes by the gravity of falling.
In the field, a cow chews its cud,
Indifferent to the idleness of the dead.

Momma cat died in the weeds,
A stink swirling in my nostrils
Until the flat hand of slapping rain
Leveled its odor. Then a neighbor died,
The one who said, Look, I got my wife's cancer—
His bony hands transparent as paper.
That was more than I needed
—mortal cat and mortal, old man—
And walked to the courthouse to sit by a pond,
Sickly fish gasping, their gills like razor slits.
Turd-coiled toads lay on the bottom, not daring to come up.
I was stirring the surface with a finger
When a suicidal cricket leaped into the pond.
Honest-to-God, I tried to save that armored insect—
My hand scooped and scooped
Like a pelican. The fish,
Sick as they were, ate antenna and spindly legs.
On the way home, I petted a stray dog,
Stared at a bird's egg cracked like a crown,
And wondered about death,
That flea-juice under my fingernail.
I grew scared. In the kitchen,
The neighbor's rooster was on the stove,
Boiling among diced celery and coins of carrots.
Do saints ever sleep? I asked my mom,
And she said, Put out the big spoons.
We ate that rooster,
Tastier than store-bought chicken.
After dinner I got Frankie's left claw
And my brother got the right claw.
We worked the tendons like pulleys
As the claws opened and closed on things—
My laughing brother picked up pencils and erasers.
Sensitive me, I went for the box of Kleenex,
Tendons closing and tissues jerking up like ghosts.

"They're gonna save us,"
I told Uncle Shorty,
A tattoo of a Chinese tiger
On his back—armed
Because war was going to happen,
Was always happening.
He had come back from Korea,
No motorcade of stars on his chest
But more mounds of muscle,
He the push-up king
On carrier *Enterprise*.
"They're gonna kill us,"
He said, not pointing
Because he had a cigarette
In one hand, a cup
Of brew in the other.
But he knew what
I was asking. He said
The ones in blue
Were the enemy
And those falling
From horses at every poor shot
Were us. I stared
At the television.
We were getting slaughtered,
Each of us falling,
The ones history
Rolled over into grassy graves,
Now subdivisions in the midwest.
"That's us?" I asked,
Crawling in his lap.
More of us fell,
And some, it seemed,
Turned their arrows on themselves,

Plugged their throats
And bellies. "They're after us,"
He said. Seven years old,
I looked into his thermos cup—
Dark wine. I laid my hand
Over Uncle's hand.
Let me have a sip, I thought.
This is going to be a long movie.

In sunlight, the banana blackened.
The tomato collapsed on the drainboard
And the lash of green onion withered.
Dust boiled over the wooden floor
And the phone rang three times,
Then stopped. Newspapers piled up
On the roof, and your favorite cat
Pranced away, its cornucopia of plenty
Pawed to an empty sack. This occurred
When the wife ran away and you were left
To scrape the label from a beer bottle,
An archaeological hunt for a deeper high.
With your brothers, you now face
A backyard fire. Wind slaps the leaves
Of the mulberry. The stars, icy teeth
In the godless sky, shift in a mouth
Bigger than any yawn you have ever seen.
Brother One says, Don't ever pee
On an electrical fence. He pokes
The fire with a stick, stomps on an ember.
Brother Two says, You can grow a full beard
Even if you're dead. He drinks
To that fortune. You scrape your bottle,
And touch your face, now stubbled,
Now curly in places. Is that what you are,
Dead and growing a beard? You kick a hot ember
And notice the fence is wood, not wire,
Not charged with the devil fire of electricity.
There is no way out. The black sky yawns,
Tired of your tears, of the paper label
Worked under your fingernails.
The stars chew the hearts of even good men.

LAZY SOULS

I'm a dog with a leash in its mouth,
A lazy soul walking its boredom around the block.
Sick, I can't push dirt under my fingernails
Or face a worm that works the earth with both head and tail.
Thus, I run a palm through the weeds.
Thus, I place the boulder of my bottom into a chair.
Thus, I smack my lips for a Japanese beer,
Lantern that lightens up any conversation.
The invisible stars crank their gears
In my favor. A friend appears,
Like a weed, and we trot off—what are we but dogs,
Filthy leashes in our mouths, then dropped.
We're too tired to carry that weighty leather.
We leap over a fourteen-inch gutter.
My friend stops. He bends to tie his shoe,
A dead brown mouse. I turn
When I hear a grunt. Across the street,
A crazy wino struggles to untwist a coat hanger,
Highly mechanical when you're starched at mid-day.
Don't hurt yourself! I scream to the wino,
The hanger now around his head.
My friend, shoes tied, says, The dude's all *rasgüachi*,
Messed up. I feel guilty,
The weeds now taller around my yellow house,
My wife with her fists white with flour.
Still, I gather the leash in my mouth.
We go to the liquor store, shoes squeaking and groaning.
Even cheap leather scolds our lazy souls.

SEVENTH GRADE SHOES
for Victor Martinez

My shoes were shapeless as rain puddles,
A clown's act, snouts of aged sharks,
Saddlebags slapped open and closed for a century.

Belly full of morning mush,
I put them on. I walked over frost-hard lawns
And understood the power of hiding—
Walk in crowds so no one will see your shoes,
Those hand-me-downs, the curled second hands in racks
At St. Vincent de Paul, the welfare saint of the poor.

I figured this:
Every seventh grader sported shoes like mine.
When I moved, the crowd moved.
When I climbed the steps, they all pushed along.
When I stopped at the drinking fountain,
They waited in a clump.
The water drooled—
Somewhere on campus a toilet was flushing
Or the showers were steaming up the eyeglasses
Of myopic fat boys.

We badly shod students moved in a great herd,
And if I ran, they tried to keep up,
This platoon of boys and girls, all shamed
By the leather on their feet.

                    Pigeons did the same,
Moving in crowds. I began to think
They too were full of shame—the shoeless creatures
Assigned to walk in gutters and peck at gum,
Dropped donuts, cigarette butts,
The debris that slips thoughtlessly from our fingers.

I felt sorry for this sad tribe
And began to dislike the jay and robin,
The cockatoo and macaw that I saw in books.
I despised those jungle birds bright as crayons,
Not like the poor pigeons the color of ash.

In my muddy shoes,
I entered the classroom with a classmate breathing
On my collar, so close that we were twins,
Conspirators. I didn't dare look down
Or dare stand up first when the bell rang.
The entire class exited shoulder to shoulder
When school let out. We seventh graders herded together
But peeled slowly away, none of us
Saying words like "good-bye" or "so long."
We parted one by one just as the sun slipped
Into the poach of winter fog.

I walked home.
When I saw a lone pigeon,
It was dead, with its claws straight in the air.
Right then, I grasped my lesson in the power of crowds,
Not like that bird, smart-aleck loner.
I nudged him with my shoe.
The wind parted its ash-colored feathers,
And, except for me, no dressed citizen really cared.

I was a werewolf, age seventeen,
Gnawing a leftover pork chop on the backporch,
My chin lost in teenage fuzz, eyebrows dark.
I looked in a hand mirror—yes, my face was bristly.

My friend Stevie rode up on his bike,
He too a werewolf, tongue red as a petal
In the cheese-chunk of his ugly face. He kicked
The kickstand down
And we sat on the porch,
Each of us sneaking quick glances into the mirror.

We did our werewolf thing—beat each other on the lawn,
Then scratched because the grass was itchy.
We drank water from the garden hose, peed
On a rose bush, and wrestled over a half-chewed Snickers,
Bellies sloshing like fish bowls. By then,
My stepfather was home, a werewolf himself,
Hairy from the tug of decades of moonlight and such.
He drank his werewolf grog at the kitchen table
And beat his fists on the table top—
Something about Republicans,
Hairless, ball-less,
But what fat wallets!

Stevie and I left on his bike,
Me bouncing on the handlebars.
Dusk. Hot enchilada dinners sifted through the sycamores,
Scenting our dirty little town with meat.
We biked to the levee—other teenage werewolves
Jumping up and down, lashing more pee into the current,
Hurling themselves against each other.

We threw the bike down.
This is A-OK, Stevie crowed
And piled onto the others, the sweat
Of his teenage years flowing among these friends.
A sensitive werewolf, I leaned a shoulder into a young tree,
And spun my shoes. Something had to come down,
Tree or this suffering. I looked skyward—
Moonlight! I stepped around the wrestling werewolves
And dragged my teenage soul through the dust,
Luring leaves and cockles, burrs and foxtails.
I howled at the godless sky.
I ran toward the moonlight on the canal,
Wild hair up my ass, some unraveling from my armpits
And groin, curly bushels on my palms,
Hair like static frying over my body.
Arms stretched out, fingers wiggling,
I ran and, like everything
I desired—girls with their peachy fuzz, dammit!—
The moon's cleanly shaved face was just out of reach.

Right away, I went to the loading dock.
Right away, I took off my hat for these people
With jobs. I said, "Hey, is Rick there?"

A Rick came out, but he wasn't my brother.
"No, Rick the Mexican," I yelled.
Another Rick came out, this one named Ricardo,
His hair black because the worst was over—
His Aztec relatives slaughtered five centuries before.

I caught on my brother wasn't on the dock,
But inside, perhaps lifting small boxes,
Perhaps with rolled sleeves and burning his eyes out
Under a fluorescent bulb. (An artist,
He could draw $ on the head of a pin.)

I walked around and entered the office,
Again with hat in hand. I asked, "Is Rick here?"
Rick came out, but again he wasn't my brother,
Only a fellow with a tie noosed around his neck,
Ready to hang.

I described him to the secretary,
Saying that he was tall, yes, dark, yes, handsome, I guess.
"He's too good to work here," she said,
Then answered a call, head thrown sideways into the phone.

She called out another guy named Rich,
Then Ray, Robert, and Ralphie,
A family of names that started with R.
But none of them was Rick my brother.
I stepped back, confused because the address was right.
I next spied the water cooler.
"Is it free?" I asked the secretary,

My body sobbing sweat from the five-mile bike ride.
I drank like a camel, filling my legs with free liquids,
Then, with back turned, dipped a finger into paper cup
And washed my eyelids of smog and insects.

My eyes dripped tears.
I left the computer factory, worried for my brother,
Who on a Monday morning walked
Into this place. By Friday,
He had disappeared.
Ricky, I called under my breath.
His name hung only inches from my face,
Then dropped. He now had a job
And a tie and a white collar
For the next thirty years. My brother with a paycheck,
With a wife and son, wasn't coming out anytime soon.

Why do you feel qualified? Mr. Blue Blazer asked,
And I looked out the skyscraper window.
Far below, a man struggled with a shopping cart,
One wheel stuck, his cargo of tin and glass jingling.

Sir, answer us, Mr. Suede-patches-at-the-elbow asked.
I stood up and peeked further down,
Pigeons flattened in the gutter,
Their feathers fossils for my own flight.

It says here you're an artist, Ms. Perfume inquired.
I gazed at my belt, lynch for the last day of the month.
I considered my fingernails,
Claws that hugged a tree for the love of its roots,
And swallowed my spit, a poor-man's breakfast.

The chairs squeaked.
The fish in the lighted salt tank circled,
A fish that I had been eyeing
Since I stepped into office.

I'm qualified because...I started.

Mr. Patches leaned forward, head like a chunk of cheese.
Ms. Perfume jangled her bracelets.
Mr. Blazer swabbed his front teeth with a sour tongue.

...because I could eat that fish in that tank there
With a butter sauce, I finished.

Out on the street with my portfolio of wrong answers,
I turned in a circle and thought, What next?
Hurrying away, nearly running from the gravity
Of a San Francisco hill,
I was every dark penny that rolled away,
But still hopeful of running into the glittery crowd
Of nickels and dimes.

In August, when a girl called
And said, I'll meet you in front of the store,
The werewolf's itch of new follicles returned.
I said, Who's this? Then the phone went dead,
And the sandwich in my hand suddenly soured.
I sat back on the couch, the TV on,
Our cat Max licking between paws
For a morsel of sparrow.

I ate cake for strength
And drank cold water.
I rode my bike to the Fresno mall,
Where I stood in front of a shoe store.
Every kind of leg walked past,
Long and short, honey brown and milky white,
Some bowed and others so tight that no nickel could pass...
I like you, I said to the world
Of girls. I like you! I like you!
I pounded my fist on the front tire,
And bounced the bike up and down.
I was strumming the spokes—an angelic music
For idiots—when the manager shooed me away.

By then, the sugar of my cake was gone,
And most of the water, now sweat, washed my face.
I kicked down to a dress shop. I walked in
And said to the tailor, Is my mom here?
He shook his head, pins in his teeth,
And I said—god knows why—that my mom was getting
Married again and she was looking to wear green,
The color of Gary Cooper's eyes,
My father's actorly name.

But by then, I was a werewolf,
My face spiked with hair. I growled,
And my stomach followed suit—seventeen, and I couldn't go
Three hours without eating.
I haunted the front of the jewelry store
And again was told to go away.

The sun put me in a headlock.
I ran a hand through the fountain
With its armada of paper cups and cigarette butts.
I muttered to a pigeon, poor fellow
With a splayed beak from pecking a dense city life.
I rode back home,
A hairball from foot to sweaty head,
A tangle of curls in the spokes and oily chain.
I was growling when I pushed open
The door at home. The phone was ringing—
Girls, I suspected, calling from the mall,
Teasing a boy who was water, fur,
And the world's oldest boomeranging bone.

WHERE WERE YOU WHEN YOU FIRST HEARD
OF AIR-CONDITIONING

How I wanted to befriend an ice cube,
Say, "My square amigo, don't leave me!
Tell me about Grandma Glacier."

How I wanted to shrink myself to the size of a fly
And sit on the lip of an ice tea.
I could careen around the rim,
My toes sweet with sugar.

How I wanted to hug a shiny, olive-black dolphin,
And say, "After the ice cube, you're my best friend."
That prankster, he'd blow water in my face,
Then cackle.

A Fresno summer. The lawns,
Green in shade, helped, but not much.
The sun rolled over us eight-to-five sinners,
We poor people paying one more time
Because we were easy targets.

The heat was a bully.
He spit on us first and then got us into headlocks.
Bored with our shine, he let go at night.

And at night the police circled the blocks,
Looking for trouble,
Or maybe a breeze that would bring on autumn.
The stars stole only so much heat from the asphalt.
Sprinklers sighed. Dogs panted.
Snails dragged their sludge toward the moonlight.

And we burros of hard labor?
Adults sat in the orange glow of a porchlight,
Reading Bibles. Was it Eygpt? Israel?
Why are boils rising on our faces and arms?
Where did we go wrong?

And me in swim trunks but no pool?
I turned the pages of *Better Homes and Gardens.*
Nice, I thought. Cool. Air-conditioning
Even in the toilet. A breeze up
Your butt when you just sat there.
O Alaska! O Tundra! O greedy Greenland
With more ice than it could use.
How the rich lived, how they whistled when they flushed,
The icy belt buckles clanging around their knees
As they raised their cool, dry-to-the-touch, jockeys.

GET OUT OF TOWN
for Juan Felipe Herrera

Blind Tiresa, pagan god of no importance,
Soother of cankers and skinned knees,
You were booted out of town by Christians,
Their bottoms gnawed by lions and such.
Zeus left two days earlier,
The crack of lightning in his rolling shoulders,
And Jupiter took a room in Florence,
Gigolo of the future.
Venus opened a beauty parlor
And clad in a hospital gown Socrates
Pushed a shopping cart for two thousand years.
But as for you, Tiresa, they were tired
Of your blind face, those cataracts
Like moons, an onion stink
In your beard. Maybe a dog followed you,
Or you followed a dog. Olive trees thinned to rock
And a sneeze of dust. Oh, you two-faced stars!
You cried, and rolled down a flint-dry hill.
You rubbed spit, atomizer of love and hate,
Into your own skinned knees.

Amigo, it still goes on—
The robed prophets still limping out of town.
Like yesterday. I led a party to the Fresno River,
A stream as thin as a wrist.
We looked at one leaf-shaped fish,
And thought, Christians planted it there.
We looked to the rocky foothills—
The lambs of kindness were gazing upon us.
On a farther hill, a sign read, Jesus.
We were scorned by crickets in the grass.
Ants bullied themselves into the rickety shade
Of mesquite and tumbleweed. Oh visible stars!

We cried at noon, Bring us lions!
But the beasts didn't show up growling.
Instead, teenagers hurled beer bottles at us,
And a redneck biker shot BBs between the gap
In his teeth. Misunderstood,
We wept as we covered our footprints.
We threw our watches into the river,
A pinch of sand in our mouths,
For what were we but dust and a canceled time?

The prof said, "It was a memorable class,"
And we applauded, none of us
Thinking of the old guy, really,
But how we, in our liquids that were mostly semen
And sweat, could get away. I gathered
My textbook, nearly unread,
A tome that I would sell because the country ran
On money, and I needed my share.
I left Economics 1, no brighter by numbers
Or national trends, and sat between two eucalyptus.
I tried to think of the Spanish verb
For shove off. After all, I was a boat
And these hard courses my choppy seas.
I let the thought go. Soon I lay on the grass
Between these mighty trees. I listened to the leaves,
Their fluttering sails, and slept
Until a dog sniffed my elbow,
A bone if I hadn't sat up and took control.
The pooch rolled his tongue, my breath
Giving off the scent of a recently eaten sandwich.
A common sight on campus,
He lived off handouts and drank from sprinkler heads,
Or licked the dewy lawns for minerals.
He studied the soft hearts of liberal arts students,
And, unlike me, knew about supply and demand.

Later, I sold my textbook
And took the cost-free excursion looking at girls.
Still later, I saw the old prof in the parking lot.
He was confused, helpless, as he searched for his car,
One hand on his ass, the snag of underwear.
I walked in front of him, the stingy bastard.
He couldn't hold a memory of his students for two hours,
We the brown pennies of his income.

Hey, Professor, I called,
And, startled, he let go of his underwear
And offered a smile that cost, really,
Just about nothing.

Something's got to happen.
Talk starts when water runs into the gutter

And two men, both leaf-blowing retirees,
Stare at this runoff, glare like a windshield at noon.

Maybe they set paws on their hips.
Maybe whiskers tremble on their stone-sharp jaws.

Maybe these Paul Bunyans step over this water
And consider the rivulet with no start nor end,

Just an occurrence under the Fresno sun.
They step back onto the curb.

One gives off a meat-scented burp.
The other jingles coins in his pocket,

The tambourine of fixed income.
Silence is an empty snail shell

Until one says, Larry's doctor told him
Bike for his health. The snail shell of silence

Swirls around them. He adds: Larry got killed
On his bike. Near Tulare Street.

These retirees, these people we're becoming,
Consider the run off, then the smoke over the trees,

Yet another wonderment when one raises a face
To the sky. Something's got to happen

Between noon and nightfall,
Something more than water and smoke,

Or even later when the moon, pale against neon
Of strip malls, rises in the east

And lights up the cemetery, a gathering place,
A sort of lake into which all neighborhood rivers run.

Can you lift
That? Hilda asked,
And I circled
The washing machine,
Circled it wide so that
I stepped slowly
Away, nearly
Across the lawn
And up the neighbor's porch.
I rubbed my chin,
A nice touch I thought.
And I thought this:
I could walk backwards
Up the block
And toward Blackstone Avenue,
So faraway that I
Could see myself
In her life,
Two kids from a previous
Marriage, one more
Behind the curtain
Of her maternity smock.
I could climb the foothills,
Burnt as the snout
Of a German Shepherd
And heavy with boulders
No river could move.
I measured her asking,
And Hilda measured me,
A young man, teeth not yet
Straight in his head.
You can do it,
She cooed, smiling,
Her smock billowing.
I looked away—

A kitten wrestled
On the lawn
And a robin
With its bib of red
Flew from the fence.
I lifted a corner
Of the washer,
Heavier than boulders.
I don't know, I said,
Spanking my palms.
She said, Sure you can,
Her hand now touching
The black, black hair
Of her oldest boy. I eyed
Hilda and my task,
Spanked my palms once more,
And moved it one corner
At a time, groaned
And sweated until
It sat on the back porch.
I was shiny as a trout,
My gills working
For air. I did my job,
Then opened the lid
Of the washer—
A load of diapers,
Which, like me,
Were ready for soap
And the rising water,
Ready to hang
In the predictable
Turn of a springtime sun.

A Junior League woman in blue
Showed me enough panty
To keep my back straight,
To keep my wine glass lifting
Every three minutes.
Do you have children? she asked.
Oh, yes, I chimed. Sip, sip.
Her legs spread just enough to stir
The lint from my eyelashes,
Just enough to think of a porpoise
Smacking me with sea-scented kisses.
The Junior League woman in yellow
Turned to the writer next to me,
Bearded fellow with two remaindered books,
His words smoldering for any goddamn reader.
This gave me time. Sip, sip,
Then a hard, undeceitful swallow
Of really good Napa Valley wine.
My mind, stung with drink,
Felt tight, like it had panty hose
Over its cranium. I thought
About the sun between delightful sips,
How I once told my older brother,
Pale vampire of psychedelic music,
That I was working on a tan.
That summer my mom thought I had worms—
I was thin as a flattened straw,
Nearly invisible, a mere vapor
As I biked up and down the block.
I rolled out an orange towel in the back yard
And the sun sucked more weight
From my body. After two hours,
My skin hollered...I let the reminiscence
Pass and reached for the bottle,

Delicately because I was in a house
With a hill view held up by cement and lumber.
A Junior League woman in red
Sat with her charming hands
On her lap, studying us two writers,
Now with the panty hose of drunkenness
Pulled over our heads and down to our eyes.
What do you do exactly, Mr. Soto?
And I looked at her blinding
Underwear and—sip, sip—said, Everything.

Perhaps Frost was poking his secretary,
The apple core of his good-living chewed
To the bitter seed. Perhaps he buttoned up,
Disgusted with the dead lizard cupped in his palm.
And his woman? She was as large as Gilbraltar,
A chunk of cheese in each armpit.
She took a deep breath
And wiggled the goose of her tasty fanny
Into the kitchen. There, she poured pancakes
Onto a skillet as old as this country,
And Frost, a pioneer for all writers,
Picked up his beaver-thrashed pencil and proclaimed,
O Sweet Youth, etc.

         I don't know how to read
Biographies, the dead words of dead writers
Etched on my eyes, then gone. I read them,
And drive my car recklessly through leaves,
The cushion for my own eventual death.
Sure, I reflect, like a chip of mirror,
And then I forget them, these subjects,
These writers with lungs and straight-A penmanship.
They're of no use. I'm not saved
By the repetitions of jealousy and all-day drinking.
Wind frisked the trees, hair fell like wheat,
And the liver, saddlebag of disease,
Bulged with inoperable knots.

I touch my own hip, then hobble home
Where a pumpkin glows in a window.
Birds shrug into their coats of dirt.
Crickets stop the violin action of their thighs.
A fire is built, and I'm lit in the living room.
I'm a democrat, I slur to the couch,
And add, Venus is a star and fly trap.
Thank God, I've learned nothing.

Two tropical flies muscle a greeting card
To the floor. They then devour dust,
Shell that is my skin, and lick each other's furry bottom.
I click my ballpoint forty-three times, my age.
I click and reread the greeting card,
Its words printed in Hong Kong. I tire of this exercise,
This irony, this spring jumping in the pen.
I get up and open the refrigerator—
A plate of pirate-crossed drumsticks
And a radish that has climbed into the skirts
Of overpriced lettuce. I drink cold water.
When I close the refrigerator,
I lean on the sink.
The flies, black as a worker's snot, hum behind me,
Their furry bottoms now reasonably clean,
Their hunger for dust more ferocious.
I can tell they are from Fresno, little drunk bastards.
I laugh and they buzz,
And I feel so dizzy that I could strangle
Every tenured philosopher in our western states.
You see, I'm a failed prof throwing away books,
March of words that never arrive.
I look east, toward the valley,
Home of rage and buried onions—
The fumes of these two curses carry on wind,
And stagger its citizens with tears
Jumping from their bleary eyes.

In time I'll be that old man in a white belt,
The three buttons of my Hawaiian shirt undone,
Gold jewelry jingling. I'm taking
My first salsa lesson,
My teacher padding about in kung-fu slippers.

"Relax," she tells me.
I can't do that, I think to myself.
To relax means that my face sags,
My belly spills to my knees,
My false teeth hang from my jaws like a Venus's-flytrap.

I press my hand to hers,
Salt to her salt. I look around—
Beginners asleep in the arms of their partners,
Panty hose twisted around ankles,
Polyester slacks puddled to shoes.

"Relax!" she scolds again.
My pompadour collapses,
My intestines sink even farther into a silken cavern,
And across the country, at that financial moment,
My mutual funds flatten to four percent.

I struggle with gravity, the mean stepsister of age.
And struggle with my teacher,
Who spins me away, then back into her arms—
Mambo kings in her hips,
The fire stomp of a cha-cha in her feet,
And timbales and trumpets going wild.
I can't keep up. She dips me like a ironing board,
Blood rushing to my head, scared that I'll fall
And be run over by the trample of the beat.

In time, I'll be that body near the fire exit,
The door nailed closed
And black smoke rising from a burning heart.

The peacock cried at the edge of a gravel road,
Its sadness the cry of a mother
Who has drowned her children
And now stumbles along a river,
The stars dipping their thorny points
Into the black rush. The peacock cried,
Then strutted back into Kearny Park.
I parked under a eucalyptus, carved
Ruthlessly with names. My car ticked.
The engine threw up a ghostly heat.
Where was La Llorona,
Outlaw woman with one shoe missing,
An entire family gone? Night in Kearny Park.
The west sucked the last light
Over the purplish hills. A plane outlined
The acres of grapes, none of them mine,
And I burned under the moon
For a Japanese girl to water my eyelashes
With a sorrowful so long. Like the fox
I could raise my chin, sniff, and see in the dark.
I could make out the peacock, now quiet,
And great sails of the eucalyptus.
We were all stirring, gnats and mosquitoes,
Bats that wheeled over the bearded coals
Of a barbecue. Gravel cooled.
Wind eased through the roadside oleanders.
Because I was young, rope thin and beautifully sad,
I followed the peacock, its cry separate
From mine but pained nevertheless
By our unmeasured walk.

Freddie's Silent Treatment toward His First and Last Wife

Freddie says he was the burro of Zen for three weeks,
While he stood tied to a pole in an August sun,
His long eyelashes gathering sand
From the beery wind of every Fresno yawn.
Flies crawled his hide, potential leather
For a failing Mexican baseball team.
Flies visited his nostrils and munched
On his ears. He let them assume their status,
And he did nothing. Zen called for that,
And he bucked his wife and horniness,
Bucked his wish for a full-time job with benefits.
He became a stone,
No, a burro, no, a stoned burro
Because three kids on bikes stopped
To hurl clods at him. From his pole,
He turned clockwise, then counter clockwise,
And let loose the stones of hot turds,
His answer to the brutality of youth.
The boys rode off, bored
Because Freddie the burro could only shit and blink,
Not sound off with a bray. He had nothing
To say to pain. He was a Zen burro, poor Freddie,
Tied to a bad marriage, the lawn mower,
And flies, those husky bastards, who kept pace
As he marched across the rocky lawn.

TALL TALE AT THE CRAM-IT-INN BAR
for C. M.

You see, there's this guy Melvin,
Fat piled up on his face
And hair receding like the sea.
This at twenty-seven, this when he limped to the bar,
One leg short. He ordered a tall draft,
Mellow lantern to lighten his talk,
Then slapped his leg for being what it was.
What luck, he said to the buds
With hair and even legs. But look at John Lennon,
He said, all hair and no fat and now he can't play
His trumpet. Guitar, a bud corrected.
Melvin clawed cigarette smoke,
Dragon in front of his face. He drank his brew
And asked, Who's the fellow with the trumpet?
Louie Armstrong, a bud said, and he's dead, too.

So this guy Melvin did math in his head,
Figured that because his leg was shorter
He would always arrive late.
Some geese were known for that,
Their wings hardly longer than the span of eyelashes.
Geese flocked in Melvin's mind
When a stranger came up and presented a card:
"Your head is not a bowling ball."
Melvin wanted to boot the stranger with his long leg,
But listened when he bought him a bottled beer.
You mean you can reshape a poor man's head?
Melvin asked. At a table,
The stranger showed pictures from an album—
All the heads reshaped, nice looking,

Even the fellow with a head thin as a business card
Coming at you,
But wide as a car door turned in profile.
The before-and-after forced Melvin to whistle.

It's a miracle, Melvin crowed, impressed
Because a second free beer foamed
In front of him. The stranger closed the album
And patted Melvin's thigh. I hear
One leg is short, he said. Melvin got up
And waddled like a duck, neck going in and out
To exaggerate the point.

Melvin evened out that day,
All because the stranger and two buds swung him
By his short leg,
Swung him dangerously close to the jukebox
And cigarette machine, over the playing field
Of the pool table. He swung Melvin
Until the skin stretched
And a bone clicked. Sure, Melvin was dizzy
After this ride around the bar,
But this, too, stopped, after the stranger
Handed him his third beer.

                    That's a damn lie,
I said to C. M., redneck poet who was soft in the heart.
I shook my head, swigged my beer, bullshit
On my boots because it's a long way to success.
You're pulling my leg, and it ain't even short!

Think what you want even whistle what you want,
But like I'm saying, bro', you going to get caught
Like the rest of us. Caught right in front
Of the headlights of a hearse, big rig for the dead.
Know what I mean? Get caught in those lights,
And don't matter if you raise your hand to block
That shine. It don't matter even if you
Jump in a tree. That old hearse climb right up
And grab your ass. You see, a hearse never get tired
Of going up and down the block, in your case *el barrio,*
And poaching young and old. *Sabes, amigo?*
Death come when you got tacos in your mouth
Or a corn dog. You just go. And what I hear
Is you get to see everything one more time,
All your school work and your teachers, the good ones
And the bad ones. All those home runs you hit,
Even the ones you didn't but bragged you did
Because you and I know your socks got more knots
Than your arms. Truth is told, *amigo!*
You hear that shit? You get one more peek
At all those legs you threw open and all those legs
Closed real quick and said, No thanks, ma'am.
Know what I mean? Sing your ass off!
Kneel in your church and roll on that dirty carpet!
But that hearse is going to find you. Like Tyrone,
A young man at a bus stop. In college and shit.
Airplane part fell out the sky and hit him on the head.
Now ain't that bad luck? Hearse slide around the
Corner and pick up Tyrone, then his mother
A week later—died with a bag of groceries
In her arms. Bad heart from what I hear
And just plain tired of carrying. You gotta go light,
The way I see. Move like cat right on a fence.
That's why they got those big-o eyes

And pads on their feet, like kung-fu slippers.
Quiet. The old hearse be looking
But won't hear your mess. Known people like that,
Soft touch on the street. They don't walk on leaves
Or step on cracks. All lived long, faces old
But better looking than those in the ground.
You hear me? Walk light, like Kung-Fu.
Stay outta bars after twelve and drink no more
Than you can pee in one long standing. And watch
The sky! Don't let no airplane fall on your head.

PETE WILSON, POOR-MAN'S DETECTIVE

He breathed in the smells of a sombrero—
Bakersfield came to mind, Porterville or Modesto,
And the whip of river where his one clue
Was a Corona beer bottle. He held it up,
Latex glove on both freckled hands.
Back in office, he clicked his pen, worried—
Yes, the Mexicans had arrived by river
Or the state's limousine, the Greyhound Bus.
Now the poor-man's detective drove from
One city to the next, all of them loud with
The wagging tongues of radios. Things
Were said, music played. Still the people
Couldn't keep up to the spin cycle of
Washing machines. These new people were
Always sick, doubling over in sweatshops,
Falling with short hoes in fields, gripping bulbs
Of cancerous spleens. It cost line-item money,
These freak accidents, these people who
Drove through red lights, gold teeth gleaming.
The poor-man's detective sniffed the sombrero—
Clue that something was up. In Fresno,
He put on that hat at the corner of G and Tulare.
He looked about—Mexicans staggering at midday,
Bottles in their hands. He licked a pencil,
Noted that poor city taken over,
Madera too, Chowchilla and Hanford.
He walked the street, a spy of sorts
With a single bullet in his breast pocket.
He was indifferent to the brown child,
A mere vapor, a mirage of heat wavering on asphalt.

He walked through the vapor, clicking his pen
And looking for trouble. Now and then
He uncovered his head, one hand on the snub
Of his inch-long bullet, and sniffed the sombrero—
Smell of something terribly, terribly wrong.

The ceiling was low,
And my ambition nearly reached its spidery cracks,
Nearly touched the bare bulb, the water mark,
A colander of holes where maybe God would slip
Through in his second coming.
I wondered how the ceiling stayed
Up there, painted and holding back rain
And the slow tractor pull of boiling clouds.
I pressed an ear to the wall,
And wasn't a wall like a ceiling,
Only upright? From the wall,
I heard rumblings of failed gods in the afterlife,
Rumblings of a muffled "oh no, oh no."
Death was like that, a permanent regret.
This scared me. If the dead lived in the walls,
Then they circled above in the ceiling,
Its ambassadors the spiders that fanned out
Their shadows in the corners. I touched my face.
Outside, a weeping neighbor with his ear to a tree.
I turned and lay on the couch. The ceiling
Was low, a coffin lid, close and nearly
Touching my nose. I slowed my breathing.
Our president with a colander of three holes.

Monsignor, I believed Jesus followed me
With his eyes, and when I slept,
An angel peeled an orange
And waited for me to wake up.
This was 1962. I was ten, small as the flame
Of a struck match, my lungs fiery
From hard, wintry play. When I returned home,
Legs hurting, I placed my hands on the windowsill
And looked out—clouds dirty as towels
And geese I have yet to see again
Darkening the western sky.

Monsignor, a machine
Had painted on the eyes of my toy soldier,
Little dots off center,
Almost on his checks. Such a cheap toy,
I drowned him over and over in my bath,
Drowned him until the painted-on eyes flaked off.
Then a leg fell off—surge of dirty water
Sunk him to the bottom.

Now, in my late forties, I place hands on the windowsill,
My eyes nearly on my cheeks,
My belly with its rising tide.
There is no angel with an orange at the edge
Of my bed. There is no soldier
Of God. Only a pane between the inside
And the outside, between this living
And this dying. Monsignor,
Saintly man of this child's wonderment,
When will I see the geese again?

I bathed my foot in an icy current
And slept with my face in sand,
Untroubled by the family eating
In their white minivan. I heard their cud
Churning, then laughter about my naked hooves
And skinny legs, those get-away sticks
That had brought me that far.
I rolled over, face in wind
And scent of hot dogs. I unbuttoned my shirt,
Hairs like crawling cilia of bacteria.
That's when the minivan pulled away.
The river was mine
Until a duck waddled up, slick as oil.
He looked at my chest with its black and white grasses,
And considered my belly,
Yet another hill to get around.
This ancient duck, its greased sockets tired of flying,
Clacked its beak and honked the breath of fish.
He stepped into the river and floated away,
South or southeast. Either direction,
He was going home. And me?
I lay on crumbled rock, late September,
The self-hatred of the river
Slowly eating its banks,
Twigs and driftwood, this body of mine.

Monsignor reminded us about the dying—
He could talk like that in his sixties,
More than half-dead and face gray as a pigeon.
I was nine, three fingers burnt from playing
With matches. I crossed myself,
Left church and walked up M Street,
A different route because the leaves
Of the sycamore were seared, unsalvageable,
Beautiful to crush in your hands and smell.
Autumn had pulled in its light,
The days growing shorter. Soon the rains
Would come to douse the fire
At the edge of my fingers,
The fire of scraped knees and elbows,
Of my mother's temper and summer's hate.
I kicked through leaves,
Picking up the scent of an earthly departure.
Then a car rounded a corner. A boy fell out
When the door swung open. The car braked,
And a frantic mother was out of the car,
And hugging the boy,
His palms and knees burned
From the slide on asphalt. Otherwise,
He was OK. The car drove away
And I crossed the street to look
To see if there was blood. Nothing,
Or almost nothing, a sweep of sand
Soaking up the grace of that moment.
I looked up. An elderly couple had stopped,
Hands on their hearts, then hurried on
To cut a path through the falling leaves.

You would read better
If you wore eyeglasses,
The nun said behind her own glare.
I was sure if I sifted for eyeglasses at Woolworth's,
My genius would spread a gospel of big words
And help explain my shoplifting.
I would snap at the cashier without eyeglasses,
"Polygenic, scalawag, my favorite osprey,"
A bullet riddle of words that would turn her inward,
Baffled, her left hand scratching the satchel
Of her buttery underarm. But if she were brave,
A tea kettle of spouting anger,
She might bounce back, "Thieving boy!"
I would have no alternative but to wheel around
On my heels in front of the double glass door
A pair of eyeglasses themselves, turn and pronounce,
"My lumbo, my generative temporal bone, homo sum!"
I would ride out of Woolworth's, clever
As pliers that bite into metal and human flesh alike,
Ride out with the hurtful glare of
Eyeglasses—"elflock," "heir apparent," "sextillion"—
For the first spinster or scholarly gent who dared
To block my free education.

From mud he came and to mud he went, age eight,
Scooping sludge into milk cartons.
He was making bricks, two at a time,
And knew that straw was what held the shape.
He stirred in these grassy flakes, plus twigs,
Some radish-like roots. He made sixteen bricks
Rounded at the edges, already old from the blast
Of a summer sun. He started his own civilization,
Then walked back and forth in a lake of water,
Stomping mud. He returned inside the house.
His brother Buster had his head inside their television,
The picture tube at the repair shop.
He drank Kool-Aid and watched Buster
Do the Three Stooges, plus someone dying,
Head wilting like an old flower. His brother tired.
Since Alfredo was small he climbed inside
The television, scrunched up fetus-like,
Mumbling with chin to chest, Hey, Buster, I'm on TV.
That lasted the length of a commercial.
He then poured himself more Kool-Aid
And saw that there were twelve glasses
Of milk, then remembered the milk cartons,
How he had poured the contents into these glasses.
Would his mom get mad? Hell, yes!
She came home and he was whipped from
One room to the next, but dinner was good.
Three days passed. Fruit and kids fell from trees.
He got a bee sting on his toe,
Then went to the backyard,
His lost civilization of bricks was
Already collapsing. Aware that mud healed stings,
He wet one brick, hosing it gently,
Then worked his foot into that muddy rectangle.
He clopped around the yard, one leg shorter.

Later he got another whipping for shoving
A rock up his nose. But dinner was good,
The steam of frijoles and arroz loosening
The ancient but ever-rising flow of muddy tears.

The punk courier got on the elevator,
Ears and eyebrows pierced, a chrome knob on his tongue,
And a Master lock hanging from his nose.

Nice day, I said to the punk,
And he said, Yeah,
Then sized up the creases in my slacks,
Sharp because I was all business—
What was I but a relic who pats his wallet
Before he leaves home,
A sort of giddy-up at the end of the millennium?

Who's got the key? I asked as the elevator went down.
He looked confused, mouth open.

To your nose, I said. Who's got the key?

The elevator fell noiselessly,
And what were we but two men, one young,
One old, on our way to the same view
Of pigeons crushed in gutters.

My new girl, he sneered, then softened as the door opened.
Shit, he said. Only nineteen, and all locked up.

The needle-thin junkie checked me in at ten.
Ash fell from her mouth, the cigarette having gone dead.
She said, Check out is when you're done.

I left with the room key wet in my hand,
Still warm from the last mule
Assigned to 230. I climbed the steps,
Unhurried because the moon was round
And would spill on my sheets all night.
But what use was a key when the door,
Lock gone, swung open. I tried the light switch
With its greasy fingerprints of hell
And sized up the bathroom—
The freebies of shampoo and mouthwash, half-empty.
I touched the one towel,
Permanently imprinted with the face
Of every redneck biker from Goshen to Tulare.
I could have talked to that face, roommate for the night.
Shit, I said, left, and threw open the curtains.
The balcony was small, too. A dead pigeon,
Its pipe cleaner of legs in the air, had spit up its seed.
I looked over the edge. A boy print on the asphalt
Where some fellow, no, a woman with smarts
Once jumped. So this was my final outpost,
Me the traveling violinist with arthritic hands
And a violin with only a single string.
Used up, my concert collar dirtied,
I returned to wash my face in the bathroom.
I had failed the night before and will fail again.
I then eyed two flies kicking in the bowl—
One climbing onto the back of the other,
The professorial ranks of state colleges suddenly clear.

Judge Fremont stared from the window, screenless
And a gateway to flies and the whining generator
Of gnats. He was angry at the new workman cottages
At the corner. His red-face housekeeper
Spat at her hot iron, spatula that starched
The already boiling air of 1921.
The tenants, mostly men, stood on their porches,
Their suspenders holding up all of California.
They sweated in their all-cotton shirts,
Their straw hats filtering the summer heat.
Judge Fremont slandered these neighbors,
White like him, but so goddamn country!
One of the men leaned in the doorway with an apple
And a pocket knife, the peel coming off neatly.
The judge told his housekeeper, "New apartments
And hicks in every window." His housekeeper
Could have ironed the judge's shirt with him in it.
Instead, she let the steam wash over her face.
The judge tied his shoes, then walked up Van Ness,
Horse droppings cold in the street,
And stopped, hands on hips, to watch a Mexican
With a hat big as a buggy wheel. Them, too,
He thought, plus the Negro who choked
A dwarf on Saturday. He smirked at the Mexican,
And, in his mind, he put away the Negro,
Low as an alligator when he got through with him.
A brew of hate and sweat soured under his arms
As he continued toward the courthouse.
There, he read and chased a fly with his hat.
Later he took a walk up M Street
Where an ice man lugged Fresno's only hope
On his shoulders, and an airplane, still novel
And worth a look, was overhead. What the judge
Didn't see was brown people at the edge of town,

All of them Catholic, married, and loving the bed,
The music of springs. At five feet nine,
The judge could only see about north
Of those workman cottages. Yes, he thought,
A new house with a lemon tree in the yard.
He felt better. The future lay before him—
The corral of decent houses, all tidy behind fences,
A wife added, children like porcelain,
And for the spice of life, but not too much,
A pitcher of buttermilk on the breakfast table.

I'm walking inside the cavern of a wino's mouth,
This pathway of eight cottages where I bedded down
And dreamed. Just married, I lived
In this place and swept dust that shifted
From the parking lot, shifted from the spinning
Velocity of bald tires. I planted grass,
And under an orange tree,
I read books—a whole village of Russians
Threw up huts and taverns inside my head.
Overfed pigeons, those bishops of the telephone lines,
Warbled and watched the sun splay my shadow
As the hours passed. The Hungarian neighbor
Watched, too. She said, Who are you in the middle
Of the day, and no work! She circled me,
A rug in her hand. She slapped the rug
Against the side of her porch, dust like rumor,
Like the hooves of horses over the Mongolian steppes.
She sneezed. She asked, You from the war?
No, I said, and told her my job was books.
I squinted from the sun and her mighty glare.
She muttered about my strong bones but lazy soul.
But where is her soul, twenty years later?
Where are the windows, now smashed,
Or the screen doors, or the garden hoses rolled
And ready for the anvil of July heat?
Where is Ed, the owner, or Ziggy, confederate son?
The roofs have flown away with the decent tenants.

I'm walking between the pitted molars of a wino.
A biker comes out of cottage number three
To stand with me on the dead lawn.
He lights up a cigarette, inhales deeply.
He swabs his teeth with a tongue
That savors neither good nor bad,

And scratches his neck, tattooed with bats.
I walk the length of the pathway, my life really.
When I turn, I tell the biker that I lived here once
When the place was nice. He blows smoke,
Considers the hierarchy of pigeons still on the line.
We got plans, he says, lifting a beer
To his face, the bats pulsating as he swallows
His brew. He flicks his cigarette
Onto the dry grass that could suck an ember
And burn in minutes. He smiles his broken teeth.
Right after sandwiches and tea, he laughs,
A sprinkler right where you're standing.

Maybe Pancho Villa's valet rode his horse
Into Arizona, over the spiky trails of tumbleweed,
Beneath a sun that was a match inches from his brow.
If so, he left behind his general and the general's bones,
Pipes for the underworld. He left behind
The war that stalled, like a train,
And the wind that blew smoke of an uncoupled locomotive.
Mules died. Horses, too, and the wells drew blood and water.
Babies touched their bellies and studied the grime
At the edge of their fingers. Fire's many teeth ate corn
And wheat fields. Crows gripped the telephone lines,
All down from Hermosillo to Guadalajara,
And drank the air of sloppy killings.

I'm thinking of those who touch the great.
What happens after the heroes die?
Do the loyal sit on porches,
Unraveling apple peels with a pocket knife.
Do they sit under trees with a board game,
Checkers or dominoes? And as for the nameless valet,
Perhaps he raised a hoe for the next thirty years
Or pushed a broom in a factory with its machinery
Of smoke and noise? Hoe or broom, he paced
Over stumbled rows or oily cement,
Or marched to the orders of a general in his heart,
Now larger, the veins root-like
And groping to take hold in this new country.

The village idiot was small, head like a radish,
And because his brain was pulpy water,
He could only stare at the señoritas,
All in white blouses and long, braided hair.

That's a good tale, Juan said, drunk,
His eyes muscled with red veins.
I then crowed, There lived a worm
Who used his ass like a straw to drink tequila.

Oh, that's another good one, Juan slurred,
Slapping dust from his pants.

Then one day a mule was playing cards
And he sneezed on a full house. This brought on the worm,
Who climbed out of the bottle and down the throat
Of a *borracho*. Idiot was watching and eating radishes,
And then everyone died because...

I woke with a *cruda,* and looked east,
The lanterns of my burned-out eyes slowly
Filling with furniture. I was at Juan's house,
Impaled on the floor, head resting next to a pair
Of barbells and a junky typewriter,
An obituary half-typed. I licked my lips
And rolled onto my belly, my brain also radish,
Pulp and polluted water.

At the toilet,
Zipper down, I beheld a worm in my fingers.
At the kitchen table, Juan was passed out before four aces.
He woke with a bray, the donkey of all drunks,
And together we smacked our dry lips.
His head was small, too, and we were neither man

Nor living myth. Hell no, we were just dumb,
Voices like gnats when the phone rang.
I answered, Woe-woe, a sort of hello,
To a señorita on the other end of pulp and water.

The shadow crawls, drunk-like, across the street,
And when I look up it's fat boy Lenny,
A six-pack swinging in the blubber under each arm.
The shadow puddles behind him, dark with bullshit.
Goin' to get me a job, he says,
And I hose my walk of ants and grass clippings.
Goin' to work for Congress, he says,
Drink for free. You ever see their noses?
Don't get that way just filibustering.
You need farm subsidies for that look.
What look? I ask, water around his feet,
Flecking his pant legs, water glaring
Under the hot sun of city-owned projects.
He pinches his nose and says, The Irish look, my man!
Ain't you listening? Good whiskey every time
They sign laws and shit. I wash off my walk,
The blood of dead afternoons,
And Lenny says that he just needs a dollar
Until he gets into Congress. After that,
It's all you can eat,
Plus girls or boys if you're into pretty boys.
I go into my pocket for that dollar,
That George Washington with an Old Boy smirk.
I spray the sidewalk, ready to hit Lenny
With a blast of water needed to wake up his lazy ass.
Yeah, I be remembering my friends, he shouts.
But suddenly Lenny begins to slide
Backwards on water and bullshit,
A big ship moving out of dry dock.
Yeah, he says, Goin' to Congress but need a drink first,
A tall 45. He looks down at his feet. Goddamm,
He crows, Goin' already and ain't even voted in.

With my garden hose turned toward his shoes,
He slides on water spiked with sunlight and dreams.
He waves a fat hand, good at hiding money,
Or rolling quarters over its knuckles,
Kingpin emptying the coffers of ordinary Joes.

Charlie, our one hope, called the *chucos* from Braly Street
To line up. Since half had been in road camp,
Shackled and such, they followed his orders
And had their faces drawn in charcoal.
These thugs went away smiling at their portraits,
And Charlie, too, went away—
Three months later he was in Paris,
Fresno still stamped on his furrowed brow
And dripping farm water behind his ears.
He walked on snow,
And ate bread and cheese. He drank coffee
At outdoor cafes, an accordion of homesickness
Living in his chest. Girls helped,
And a *vin ordinaire* dark as the Middle Ages.
He studied the art of the time.
The river cracked its dull mirror of ice,
And suddenly in a heatless room
He was going abstract, the chairs no longer chairs
But buckled wood and juts of timber.
He painted a Nazi with a boot for a head
And a cathedral leaning in an atomic wind.

The river thawed from hot human tears.
The fish drank that brew and hopped onto dinner plates,
This according to Charlie's suddenly cubist art.
Back in Fresno, he showed the *chucos*
His new art, the crooked lines, the negative space,
And every face beautifully out of whack.
The *chucos* couldn't figure,
Charlie's drawing so good just months before
And now the eyes of farmers dripping like eggs.

Was he now a wino? A myopic young man?
Had existentialism weakened his blood?
My uncle looked over Charlie's fingers—
Poor guy, no telling when a train ran them over.

How I love Mexican women with mascara,
Dark apocalypse over their eyes,
The eyelashes built up with boulders
Of black. When they cry,
The boulders fall on their cheeks,
Mild avalanche that rumbles in my heart.
That's why I'm watching *telenovelas*—
An actress is leaning against a door
With tears. The boulders tumble,
And she bites a knuckle, serrated grief
She'll take to bed. She stomps
A dainty foot and cries, *No puedo! No puedo!*
The most real emotion I'll get this week.
I turn off the TV and pad to the kitchen,
Wife gone, daughter and cat gone.
What's next but to stare at the lunch meat
In the refrigerator, meat
Of pig trotters and cows hooves,
The innards of penguins and mallards,
Gizzards of bears coaxed from pine trees?
What have I been eating that I like such women?
Or think that the lunch meat,
Punched by machines and sucked into a vacuum
Of plastic, is exotic. O Carolina
With your smudge of black, O Mona
And O Carmen with boulders on your cheeks.
I sob over a dead plant with its tombstones
Of crushed cigarette butts. My tears,
Straight from the heart, won't make its leaves breathe
The exhaust of self-pity ever again.

MEAT AND POTATOES
for Carolyn

The steak was tougher than I thought,
A vest of gristle that could keep back an arrow,
Or, if stretched, pull a car down
The street, something that I did that morning,
The poor Rambler, engine dead,
Radiator wounded and tires smooth as a baby's thigh,
But still gobbling up gnats on its windshield.
To meet rent, I hauled it to the junkyard
And then bought a steak at Safeway.
I sawed through that meat, table wobbling,
Red pout on my steaming face. I rested,
The tomato with its gashed teeth grinning at me.
I ate the tomato, then turned to the potatoes,
Cool as the hands of the woman I wanted
To hold. I picked up one of the potatoes,
Still in its jacket, and cooed,
You have nice skin. I squeezed the potato, lightly,
And I answered for that veggie, That's sweet.
I looked out the window. The potato
Lived next door. I mean, the woman I loved
Lived there, and at ten to six she stir fried
Something Chinese. The flavors drifted
And steamed my window.
My nostrils flared, ready to burst like a potato.
I sighed and considered my own meal. The steak
Was still warm from its previous life.
I tried to cut it into chewable pieces,
But it was tougher than me.
Exhausted, I turned to the potatoes,
Pliable as that neighbor I would soon know.
A good boy, I ate everything on my plate,
Even the steak, and with my jaw tired,
I pounded the table with my bloody fork,

Its teeth bent and some of my own hurting.
I looked out the window. Love was at her table,
A fork going to her mouth and the noodles,
How delicious, easy to swallow.

You woke first
And rocked the back of your dog,
Main actor in your first feature.
The dog opened a bloody eye, closed that eye,
And opened the other, cleaner but still horrible
To behold. Come on! you called
And the dog rolled onto its back, paws in the air,
Churned once, and died. Since the dog was what it was,
Stray from the street, the life
Of your nappy companion passed quickly before your eyes.
Your feature film was ruined.
The footage suddenly spilled at your feet
And snarled around your knees.
The footage contained romance, but not much,
And two takes of you patting alcohol where no cut existed,
Plus repeated scenes of you parting with a French fry,
Your one act of charity. Mostly, the film
Revolved around the dog, hero of both man and animal,
Dog who invented the sprinkler and the Frisbee,
Who championed the rights of sheep,
Who founded kennels and washed the homeless,
And who was trustee for Guide Dogs for the Despondent.
The bastard did everything! He even died that morning
So that you could find yourself. You rocked his belly,
But he wouldn't move. With so much footage,
With so much to say, you carried on.
You let out a single bark and rolled off the bed.
Three fleas gripped your hair. You didn't mind.
You crawled out of the bedroom, ready
To live up to the dog's part, your knees scuffed,
Nose flared as you picked up where he left off—
The trail of romance and the spray of every beast,
Who gallantly lifted a sturdy leg
To mark a place in life.

Gary Soto

Photo: Jay Blakesberg

Gary Soto is a poet, playwright, essayist, and author of several children's books. Widely anthologized, he is a frequent contributor to such literary magazines as the *Ontario Review, Crazy Horse,* the *Iowa Review,* and *Poetry,* which has honored him with both the Bess Hokin and Levinson Prizes. He has received the Discovery-*The Nation* Award, the Andrew Carnegie Medal for Film Excellence, the Silver Medal from the Commonwealth Club of California, and an American Book Award from the Before Columbus Foundation, as well as fellowships from the Guggenheim Foundation, the National Endowment for the Arts, and the California Arts Council. A National Book Award Finalist for *New and Selected Poems* (Chronicle Books), Gary Soto divides his time between Berkeley and his hometown of Fresno.